A Beginning-to-Read Book

Needs and Wants

by Mary Lindeen

NORWOOD HOUSE PRESS

DEAR CAREGIVER, The *Beginning to Read—Read and Discover* books provide emergent readers the opportunity to explore the world through nonfiction while building early reading skills. The text integrates both common sight words and content vocabulary. These key words are featured on lists provided at the back of the book to help your child expand his or her sight word recognition, which helps build reading fluency. The content words expand vocabulary and support comprehension.

Nonfiction text is any text that is factual. The Common Core State Standards call for an increase in the amount of informational text reading among students. The Standards aim to promote college and career readiness among students. Preparation for college and career endeavors requires proficiency in reading complex informational texts in a variety of content areas. You can help your child build a foundation by introducing nonfiction early. To further support the CCSS, you will find Reading Reinforcement activities at the back of the book that are aligned to these Standards.

Above all, the most important part of the reading experience is to have fun and enjoy it!

Sincerely,

Shannon Cannon

Shannon Cannon, Ph.D.
Literacy Consultant

Norwood House Press
Chicago, Illinois
For more information about Norwood House Press please visit our website at
www.norwoodhousepress.com or call 866-565-2900.
© 2020 Norwood House Press. Beginning-to-Read™ is a trademark of Norwood House Press.
All rights reserved. No part of this book may be reproduced or utilized in any form or by any means without written permission from the publisher.

Editor: Judy Kentor Schmauss
Designer: Sara Radka

Photo Credits:
Getty Images, 2–11, 14–19, 23, 27; Shutterstock, 1, 12–13, 20, 24, 28

Library of Congress Cataloging-in-Publication Data
Names: Lindeen, Mary, author.
Title: Needs and wants / by Mary Lindeen.
Description: Chicago, Illinois : Norwood House Press, [2020] |
    Series: A beginning-to-read book | Audience: 5-8. | Audience: K to 3.
Identifiers: LCCN 2018054645 | ISBN 9781684509355 (hardcover) |
    ISBN 9781684044337 (pbk.) | ISBN 9781684044382 (ebook)
Subjects: LCSH: Basic needs—Juvenile literature. | Consumption (Economics)—Juvenile literature.
Classification: LCC HC79.B3 L56 2020 | DDC 306.3—dc23
LC record available at https://lccn.loc.gov/2018054645

Hardcover ISBN: 978-1-68450-935-5
Paperback ISBN: 978-1-68404-433-7

Good morning!

It's time for breakfast.

Your body **needs** food after sleeping all night.

What do you **want** to eat?

People need things to stay alive.

We all need food, water, clothing, and shelter.

People also want things.

We may want certain kinds of food.

We may want certain kinds of clothes.

There's a difference between needs and wants.

You **need** to breathe air.

You **want** to play soccer.

Every person has needs and wants.

But not every person has all of the **same** needs and wants.

If you live here, you
don't need snow boots.

But if you live here,
you **do** need them!

If you live here, you
don't need a boat.

But if you live here, you **do** need one!

It's important to have the things you need.

Getting what you need often costs money.

It's fun to have things you want, too.

But getting things you want can also cost money.

People have to use some of their money to buy the things they need.

If people have
enough money
left, they can buy
some things they
want, too.

Everyone has needs and wants!

What do you need?

What do you want?

. . . READING REINFORCEMENT. . .

CRAFT AND STRUCTURE

To check your child's understanding of this book, recreate the following chart on a sheet of paper. Read the book with your child, and then help him or her fill in the chart using what they learned about needs and wants. In the left column, help your child list things he or she needs, and in the right column, help your child list things he or she wants. Then discuss why each item on the list is a need or a want.

Needs	Wants

VOCABULARY: Learning Content Words

Content words are words that are specific to a particular topic. All of the content words in this book can be found on page 32. Use some or all of these content words to complete one or more of the following activities:

- Help your child sort the words into different categories. Ask him or her to tell how they sorted the words.

- Have your child make word cards to help him or her remember the words' meanings. On each word card, write the word, draw a picture, write a reminder word, and write a sentence using the word.

- Write the words and their definitions on separate index cards. Turn the cards facedown in two groups (words and definitions) and have your child turn over one card in each group until he or she finds a word and its matching definition.

- Help your child find the words in a dictionary and read the definitions. Then ask your child to use his or her own words to state the definitions.

- Provide your child with 2–3 hints about the meaning of the word and have him or her guess the word.

FOUNDATIONAL SKILLS: Consonant digraphs

Consonant digraphs are two consonants that together make a single sound (for example, *ph* in *phone*). Have your child identify the consonant digraphs in the list below. Then help your child find the words with consonant digraphs in this book.

photo	mist	reach	stuck
weather	Peter	thick	rip
rough	whine	ship	city

CLOSE READING OF INFORMATIONAL TEXT

Close reading helps children comprehend text. It includes reading a text, discussing it with others, and answering questions about it. Use these questions to discuss this book with your child:

- What's the difference between a need and a want?

- Why is shelter a need and not a want?

- Can you need something and want it at the same time? Why or why not?

- What is your most important need? Why is it a need?

- Are needs or wants more important? Why?

- What is one way to get a "want" if you don't have the money to buy it?

FLUENCY

Fluency is the ability to read accurately with speed and expression. Help your child practice fluency by using one or more of the following activities:

- Reread the book to your child at least two times while he or she uses a finger to track each word as it is read.

- Read a line of the book, then reread it as your child reads along with you.

- Ask your child to go back through the book and read the words he or she knows.

- Have your child practice reading the book several times to improve accuracy, rate, and expression.

··· Word List ···

Needs and Wants uses the 76 words listed below. *High-frequency words* are those words that are used most often in the English language. They are sometimes referred to as sight words because children need to learn to recognize them automatically when they read. *Content words* are any words specific to a particular topic. Regular practice reading these words will enhance your child's ability to read with greater fluency and comprehension.

High-Frequency Words

a	do	if	same	too
after	eat	left	some	use
air	every	may	the	want(s)
all	for	not	their	water
also	get(ing)	of	them	we
and	good	often	they	what
between	has	one	things	you
but	have	people	time	your
can	here	play	to	

Content Words

alive	certain	everyone	money	snow
boat	clothes	food	morning	soccer
body	clothing	fun	need(s)	stay
boots	cost(s)	important	night	there's
breakfast	difference	it's	person	
breathe	don't	kinds	shelter	
buy	enough	live	sleeping	

··· About the Author

Mary Lindeen is a writer, editor, parent, and former elementary school teacher. She has written more than 100 books for children and edited many more. She specializes in early literacy instruction and books for young readers, especially nonfiction.